The
FARTING DINOSAURS

Coloring Book

Coloring Pages for Kids

Coloring Pages for Kids
Published by Ciparum LLC

The Farting Dinosaurs Coloring
Book © 2016 Ciparum LLC
All rights reserved.
ISBN-10:1-63589-823-4
ISBN-13:978-1-63589-823-1

www.coloringpagesforkids.co

FART!

FART!

FART!

FART!

FART!

www.ingramcontent.com/pod-product-compliance
Lightning Source LLC
Chambersburg PA
CBHW081259310326
41914CB00110B/898